The 2-8-2 Tank Papers

7200 2-8-2Ts, 7200-7253

IAN SIXSMITH
Tables by Richard Derry

The GWR 'shirt button' was introduced in 1934 and was thus contemporaneous with the 2-8-2Ts so this, on green, appeared early on, though GREAT WESTERN in serif came first. At some point the 7200s must have emerged in green with the 'shirt button' rather than the lettering, looking like 7244 here at Landore on 28 May 1939.

Irwell Press Ltd.

Acknowledgements

Gavin Glenister, Brian Penney, Allan C. Baker, Nick Deacon, Rob Kinsey, Tony Wright and especially Eric Youldon. Richard Derry once again painstakingly compiled the Allocation Tables.

First published in the United Kingdom in 2017,
by Irwell Press Limited, 59A, High Street, Clophill,
Bedfordshire MK45 4BE
Tel: 01525 861888
www.irwellpress.com

The 2-8-2 Tank Papers
7200-7253

The Great Depression came to an end in 1933 though of course its malign effects took much longer to abate in depressed areas that relied on heavy industry like coal and steel. Existing engines had continued to age though and even with 2-8-0Ts going into traffic from store, new power was still needed. It was then that the original notion of a 2-8-2T (before a 2-8-0T configuration was decided on) was revived. Concerns about excessive length were now no longer so important, for it was envisaged that the new engines would spend their time on longer distance coal trains into England, rather than being confined to the winding Valley lines. See, of course, *The 2-8-0 Tank Papers, 4200 and 5200 2-8-0Ts, 4200-4299, 5200-5294*

So it was that from 1934 through to 1939 fifty-four 2-8-0Ts were rebuilt with extended bunker and a radial axle, with coal and water capacity substantially increased. A 2-8-0T held 4 tons 2 cwt/1,800 gallons, a 2-8-2T 6 tons/2,500 gallons.

The first engines were 7200-7219 of 1934, converted from 5275-5294, followed by 7220-7239 converted from 5255-5274. The first twenty bore the curved running plate over the cylinders of the original engines. The latter twenty inherited the straight running plates of the particular engines from which they had been rebuilt, but 7221 and 7228 later received a raised platform and curved drop.

The final engines were converted in 1937-1939 from a number of 4200 engines, which were rather older than the converted 5200 engines of course. The work involved new curved front ends and new cylinders with outside steam pipes. Coal capacity was reduced to 5 tons and water capacity increased to 2,700 gallons.

A visitor to Swindon Works in December 1939 would have seen 2-8-2T 7253 being created from 2-8-0T 4245 and new 2-8-0T 5255 coming into the world! He might have wondered if Swindon's left hand knew what its right hand was doing…

ATC

ATC was already widespread when the 2-8-2T conversions were made and with their wider sphere of work they were equipped from the first.

Power/Route Classification

Power class E, red disc route availability; BR 8F.

Livery

'Middle chrome green' would have been applied to the engines at first, for black was unknown on the GWR before the Second World War. Black was applied 1942-45 and green appeared for a few years – 7236 for instance in 1946 – including for the early months of 1948.

GREAT WESTERN in serif was the first lettering though the GWR 'shirt button' of 1934 was presumably applied to later engines as they were turned out. GWR appeared after the War, then BRITISH RAILWAYS, first in serif and then Gill sans.

The late 1948 plain black was applied with the first BR emblem from mid-1949 and the second one from about mid-1957. Throughout their lives the 7200 liveries paralleled the 2-8-0Ts. Just one 2-8-2T received the short-lived 'W' suffix and that was 7213.

7237 fairly anonymous in green with no trace of tankside lettering or insignia, probably about 1936 during the engine's time at Oxley. The location is not recorded but Rob Kinsey ventures this: I believe that it's Leamington Spa looking east, but cannot be 100% sure. The track layout looks correct as do the houses/buildings to the left of the loco; the station canopy above the centre of the train and signal box above the rear of the train also appear to match. The ex-LNWR and LMS signals would be those controlling the nearby Avenue station. If the location is correct the train is a down Class H working, heading towards Birmingham and Wolverhampton. I'd suggest that the date is 1936 as the loco looks clean (new) but I can't see any emblem/lettering/roundel on the tank side. The trees look to be in leaf so it is probably spring/summer. The leading van is in pre-1937 LNER livery. Michael Boakes Collection.

Dates of rebuilding from 2-8-0Ts		
2-8-2T	Date	2-8-0T
7200	8/34	5275
7201	8/34	5276
7202	9/34	5277
7203	9/34	5278
7204	9/34	5279
7205	10/34	5280
7206	10/34	5281
7207	10/34	5282
7208	10/34	5283
7209	11/34	5284
7210	11/34	5285
7211	11/34	5286
7212	9/34	5287
7213	9/34	5288
7214	9/34	5289
7215	11/34	5290
7216	11/34	5291
7217	9/34	5292
7218	11/34	5293
7219	10/34	5294
7220	9/35	5255
7221	9/35	5256
7222	10/35	5257
7223	10/35	5258
7224	11/35	5259
7225	10/35	5260
7226	11/35	5261
7227	11/35	5262
7228	12/35	5263
7229	8/35	5264
7230	12/35	5265
7231	12/35	5266
7232	8/35	5267
7233	9/35	5268
7234	9/35	5269
7235	1/36	5270
7236	1/36	5271
7237	1/36	5272
7238	2/36	5273
7239	2/36	5274
7240	8/37	4239
7241	9/37	4220
7242	9/37	4202
7243	1/38	4204
7244	3/38	4216
7245	5/38	4205
7246	7/38	4234
7247	9/38	4244
7248	10/38	4249
7249	11/38	4209
7250	2/39	4219
7251	3/39	4240
7252	4/39	4210
7253	12/39	4245

Proof that the GWR 'roundel' or even 'shirt button' (a triumph of the 'less is more' school of design by the way) could survive even on a 2-8-2T, with all the neglect of cleaning that implies. 7228 is at Tyseley (only one – longitudinal – boiler grab iron at this early period, and tall bonnet) in June 1937, some eighteen months after conversion from 5263. 7228 is from the second batch and retains for the present the straight running plate over the cylinders that its progenitor, 5263, was equipped with. transporttreasury

7208 hurries a northbound train of wooden wagons, constituting a class E goods, in Harbury cutting. The running plate is raised above the cylinder with a drop curve at the front, a feature inherited from the batch of 2-8-0Ts (5275-5294) from which the first twenty 2-8-2Ts were derived. A vestige of serif GWR is there under the grime, denoting the late 1940s and the train itself is a joy, with hardly any wagon matching the shape, height or outline of the one next to it. Coupling not properly stowed out of the way to protect the ATC apparatus. Michael Boakes Collection.

How it was supposed to look, with coupling correctly stowed too. 7240 at Swindon newly overhauled and beautifully painted green with GWR serif, 4 July 1947. They only look this good of course, in preservation. The secondary grab irons on the boiler have appeared, the front lamp iron is on the smokebox door not the smokebox top. GWR code OXY indicating its home shed Oxley stencilled on valence above cylinder. Still with tall bonnet but no sign, so far, of the horizontal tank weld. Note difference in rainstrips between this one and 7205 below. H.C. Casserley, courtesy R.M. Casserley.

7205 at Swindon on 16 August 1936, on the reception line outside the vast AE Shop; shortly it will be moved to the traverser to be received in the works for its first major attention since conversion from 2-8-0T 5280 nearly two years before. No lettering or emblem visible and as yet no horizontal weld line on the tank, which has a double line of rivets at the bottom near the front this side, as found on some 2-8-0T examples. Like the Big Prairies and the 2-8-0Ts, the 7200 engines had a third water tank, under the coal space; the sloping line of rivets on the bunker mark the 'roof' of the water space while behind the steps is the square-section 'equalising' or levelling pipe connecting the bunker tank with the side tank. There was obviously another one on the other side. Now, these booklets are arranged to be read in sequence, but of course they need to 'stand alone' too, so some features have to be gone over again... *The levelling pipe was secured with a rubber joint between the rectangular mating surfaces and bolts which passed down from the inside of the tanks with fibre washers and nuts tightened against the pipe flanges. These bolts frequently worked loose, causing leakage, and tightening them was difficult as the bolts tended to turn inside the tank. A regular job for an apprentice was to drop down into the tank through the filler hole and crawl along to the levelling pipe, to hold the bolt heads with a spanner while a fitter tightened the nuts on the outside. The bunker tank joint was not too difficult to work on as there was a removable plate which gave access to the joint.* H.C. Casserley, courtesy R.M. Casserley.

7200 Allocation

7200 (5275) 30/8/34; Llanelly 22/9/34; Newton Abbot 22/2/47; St Blazey 23/2/52; Landore 29/11/52; Duffryn Yard 18/6/60; Llanelly 8/10/60; withdrawn 2/7/63; mileage 605,523; sold to Woodham Brothers 9/10/63; locomotive preserved

7201 (5276) 31/8/34; Llanelly 22/9/34; Carmarthen 20/10/34; Cardiff Canton 5/2/38; St Philips Marsh 14/7/51; Cardiff Canton 11/1/55; Pontypool Road 26/2/55; Newport Ebbw Jct 20/7/64; Llanelly 5/10/64; withdrawn 21/4/65; mileage at 28/12/63 610,824; sold to Birds, Bynea 2/6/65

7202 (5277) 5/9/34; Newport Ebbw Jct 22/9/34; Gloucester 4/43; Severn Tunnel Jct 29/12/45; Cardiff Radyr 20/3/48; Barry 8/9/62; withdrawn 1/6/64, later advised as 13/6/64; mileage at 28/12/63 641,851; sold to Woodham Brothers 17/7/64; locomotive preserved

7203 (5278) 11/9/34; Newport Ebbw Jct 22/9/34; Llanelly 26/3/55; Aberdare 28/11/59; Carmarthen 24/3/62; Newport Ebbw Jct 23/2/63; Severn Tunnel Jct 5/9/63; withdrawn 16/12/63; mileage 566,635; sold to A King Norwich 28/2/64

7204 (5279) 14/9/34; Cardiff Canton 20/10/34; Llanelly 7/41; Slough 15/6/46; Didcot 22/3/47; Llanelly 2/10/48; Neath 27/1/51; Hereford 16/5/53; Pontypool Road 26/2/55; Newport Ebbw Jct 31/10/59; Aberdare 20/4/63; Duffryn Yard 11/7/63; withdrawn 26/2/64; mileage at 28/12/63 619,874; sold to R S Hayes Bridgend 24/4/64

7205 (5280) 17/10/34; Aberdare 17/11/34; Cardiff Radyr 20/3/48; Aberdare 9/1/65; Pontypool Road 6/3/65; Severn Tunnel Jct 15/4/65; withdrawn 16/6/65; mileage at 28/12/63 645,930; sold to Steel Supply Co. Briton Ferry

7206 (5281) 15/10/34; Llanelly 17/11/34; Pontypool Road 5/3/38; Severn Tunnel Jct 13/6/59; Pontypool Road 29/12/62; Newport Ebbw Jct 4/5/64; withdrawn 6/7/64; mileage at 28/12/63 536,058; sold to R S Hayes Bridgend 24/8/64

7207 (5282) 24/10/34; Severn Tunnel Jct 17/11/34; Llanelly 7/41; Oxley 17/5/47; Landore 14/6/52; Banbury 18/6/60; withdrawn 11/64; cut up at Banbury shed by J Friswells Ltd Banbury 1/65

7208 (5283) 29/10/34; Severn Tunnel Jct 17/11/34; Aberbeeg 9/1/37; Tondu 3/4/37; Severn Tunnel Jct 29/5/37; Westbury 12/41; Newton Abbot 12/43; Llanelly 2/45; St Philips Marsh 17/5/47; Leamington Spa 24/1/48; Oxley 1/12/51; Cardiff Canton 29/11/52; Newport Ebbw Jct 27/12/52; Severn Tunnel Jct 9/8/53; Banbury 3/12/60; Barry 8/9/62; withdrawn 20/4/64; mileage at 28/12/63 590,689; sold to Birds Risca 3/6/64

7209 (5284) 6/11/34; Severn Tunnel Jct 17/11/34; Newport Ebbw Jct 4/40; Severn Tunnel Jct 5/40; St Blazey 15/7/50; Landore 14/10/52; Duffryn Yard 18/6/60; Cardiff Canton 13/8/60; Oxford 10/9/60; Neath 6/10/62; Aberdare 29/12/62; Barry 29/6/64; withdrawn 24/7/64; mileage at 28/12/63 606,299; sold to R S Hayes Bridgend 4/9/64

7210 (5285) 1/11/34; Severn Tunnel Jct 17/11/34; Cardiff Canton 9/9/50; Newport Ebbw Jct 17/5/52; Pontypool Road 22/2/58; withdrawn 30/4/65; mileage at 28/12/63 612,913; sold to Birds Risca 2/6/65

7211 (5286) 16/11/34; Newport Ebbw Jct 15/12/34; Swansea East Dock 30/4/38; Llanelly 7/41; Swansea East Dock 12/41; Cardiff Cathays 2/45; Swansea East Dock 3/45; Landore 2/10/48; Llanelly 24/1/53; Newport Ebbw Jct 5/9/59; Llanelly 8/10/60; Severn Tunnel Jct 4/5/64; withdrawn 6/5/64; mileage at 28/12/63 620,070; sold to G Cohen Morriston 22/6/64

7212 (5287) 18/9/34; Newport Ebbw Jct 20/10/34; Tondu 8/2/36; Newport Ebbw Jct 28/5/37; Cardiff Cathays 12/11/38; Newport Ebbw Jct 10/12/38; Oxford 11/7/53; Newport Ebbw Jct 16/6/56; Severn Tunnel Jct 10/9/60; Aberbeeg 23/2/63; Aberdare 31/10/63; withdrawn 14/2/64; mileage at 28/12/63 594,371; sold to R S Hayes Bridgend 24/4/64

7213 (5288) 24/9/34; Cardiff Canton 20/10/34; Severn Tunnel Jct 11/12/37; Newport Ebbw Jct 30/4/38; Aberdare 5/42; Oxley 3/12/60; Llanelly 1/12/62; withdrawn 7/9/64; mileage at 28/12/63 568,159; sold to Birds Morriston 14/10/64

7214 (5289) 26/9/34; Swansea East Dock 20/10/34; Cardiff Canton 28/5/38; Didcot 13/7/46; Cardiff Canton 2/10/48; Tondu 27/11/48; Newport Ebbw Jct 28/1/50; Aberdare 17/5/58; Newport Ebbw Jct 17/6/61; Neath 2/12/62; Aberdare 29/12/62; withdrawn 16/12/63; mileage 577,206; sold to Birds Morriston 28/2/64

7215 (5290) 16/11/34; Pantyffynon [sub to Llanelly] 15/12/34; Cardiff Cathays 5/2/38; Llanelly 30/4/38; St Philips Marsh 17/5/47; Pontypool Road 24/1/48; Newport Ebbw Jct 25/12/48; Llanelly 5/9/53; Swansea East Dock 25/1/58; Danygraig 21/2/59; Swansea East Dock 3/10/59; withdrawn 24/6/63; mileage 552,035; cut up 7/9/63

7216 (5291) 23/111/34; Swindon 15/12/34; Aberbeeg 5/2/38; Severn Tunnel Jct 30/4/38; Cardiff Canton 24/3/51; Aberdare 19/4/52; Duffryn Yard 24/2/62; withdrawn 7/10/63; mileage at 28/12/63 599,720; sold to R S Hayes Bridgend 1/1/64

7217 (5292) 28/9/34; Newport Ebbw Jct 20/10/34; Aberbeeg 11/12/37; Tondu 5/2/38; Aberbeeg 5/3/38; Newport Ebbw Jct 28/5/38; Landore 14/6/52; Banbury 13/6/59; Oxley 3/10/59; Newport Ebbw Jct 26/12/59; Banbury 3/12/60; Severn Tunnel Jct 25/2/61; Newport Ebbw Jct 29/12/62; Cardiff Radyr 13/6/63; Llanelly 11/7/63; Aberbeeg 29/6/64; withdrawn 6/7/64; mileage at 28/12/63 560,016; sold to R S Hayes Bridgend 24/8/64

7218 (5293) 30/11/34; Swindon stock 15/12/34; Banbury 9/3/35; Leamington Spa 3/42; Oxley 1/12/51; Duffryn Yard 12/7/52; Newport Ebbw Jct 29/11/52; Oxford 30/1/60; Oxley 3/12/60; Banbury 1/12/62; withdrawn 8/64; sold to Cohens Kettering

7219 (5294) 10/10/34; Cardiff Canton 20/10/34; Oxley 5/3/38; Cardiff Canton 28/5/38; Newport Ebbw Jct 27/2/54; Cardiff Radyr 13/6/63; withdrawn 22/1/64; mileage at 28/12/63 620,919; sold to J Cashmore Newport 24/3/64

7220 (5255) 17/9/35; Pontypool Road 19/10/35; Carmarthen 8/1/38; Llanelly 30/4/38; Newton Abbot 22/3/47; St Blazey 23/2/52; Newton Abbot 9/8/52; Newport Ebbw Jct 1/11/52; Severn Tunnel Jct 24/4/54; Pontypool Road 11/9/54; withdrawn 7/9/64; mileage at 28/12/63 567,847; sold to J Cashmore Newport 14/10/64

7221 (5256) 25/8/35; Pontypool Road 19/10/35; Newport Ebbw Jct 5/3/38; Aberdare 8/42; Newton Abbot 4/44; Aberdare 12/44; Barry 8/9/62; Banbury 28/12/63; withdrawn 11/64; sold to J Friswells Banbury

7222 (5257) 15/10/35; Cardiff Canton 16/11/35; Aberbeeg 8/1/38; Cardiff Canton 5/2/38; Westbury 2/42; Newton Abbot 10/43; Llanelly 2/45; Oxley 17/5/47; Worcester 26/2/49; Neath 16/6/51; Llanelly 1/12/51; Neath 21/2/53; Hereford 16/5/53; Newport Ebbw Jct 6/11/55; Duffryn Yard 29/12/62; Aberdare 31/12/63; withdrawn 15/1/65; mileage at 28/12/63 558,062; sold to J E Woodfield Newport 3/1/65

7223 (5258) 10/10/35; Cardiff Canton 19/10/35; Newport Ebbw Jct 23/7/38; Gloucester 3/43; Severn Tunnel Jct 29/12/45; Newport Ebbw Jct 7/10/61; Barry 11/7/63; Llanelly 28/11/63; withdrawn 13/11/64; mileage at 28/12/63 606,294; sold to R S Hayes Bridgend 12/1/65

7224 (5259) 2/11/35; Pontypool Road 16/11/35; Swansea East Dock 31/10/53; Llanelly 15/6/57; Aberdare 28/11/59; Exeter 17/6/61; Newport Ebbw Jct 2/12/61; withdrawn 6/12/62; mileage at 28/12/63 672,533; sold to R S Hayes Bridgend 26/8/63

7225 (5260) 28/10/35; Llanelly 16/11/35; Pantyffynon 30/5/36; Llanelly 25/7/36; Landore 9/8/47; Llanelly 11/8/51; Swansea East Dock 25/1/58; Worcester 22/2/58; Danygraig 21/2/59; Swansea East Dock 28/11/59; Llanelly 23/2/62; Severn Tunnel Jct 4/5/64; withdrawn 6/5/64; mileage at 28/12/63 563,395; sold to Birds Risca 22/6/64

7226 (5261) 23/11/35; Oxford 14/12/35; Croes Newydd 2/5/36; Oxley 19/9/36; Stafford Road 21/8/37; Oxley 18/9/37; Neath 1/11/52; Swansea East Dock 29/11/52; Llanelly 15/6/57; Swansea East Dock 25/1/58; Danygraig 21/3/59; Swansea East Dock 27/2/60; Severn Tunnel Jct 31/12/63; Aberdare 7/11/64; withdrawn 13/11/64; mileage at 28/12/63 564,157; sold to Woodham Brothers 12/1/65

7227 (5262) 27/11/35 Banbury 14/12/35; Oxley 5/3/38; Neath 3/2/40; Carmarthen 1/42; Llanelly 3/43; Oxley 17/5/47; Newport Ebbw Jct 27/12/52; Barry 19/4/58; Pontypool Road 16/5/59; withdrawn 24/6/63; mileage 551,775; sold to R S Hayes Bridgend 1/1/64

7228 (5263) 14/12/35; Severn Tunnel Jct 11/1/36; Gloucester 8/40; Severn Tunnel jct 8/41; Didcot 15/6/46; Llanelly 2/10/48; Banbury 27/2/60; Severn Tunnel Jct 9/9/61; Barry 8/9/62; withdrawn 29/7/63; mileage 594,499; sold to R S Hayes Bridgend 1/1/64

7229 (5264) 24/8/35; Severn Tunnel Jct 21/9/35; Cardiff Cathays 21/8/37; Severn Tunnel Jct 18/9/37; Newport Ebbw Jct 2/3/40; Severn Tunnel Jct 30/3/40; Newport Ebbw Jct 24/4/54; Duffryn Yard 24/2/62; Neath 13/4/63; Newport Ebbw Jct 29/6/64; withdrawn 10/8/64; mileage at 28/12/63 609,338; sold to Woodham Brothers 29/9/64 - preserved

7230 (5265) 13/12/35; Severn Tunnel Jct 11/1/36; Cardiff Cathays 18/9/37; Severn Tunnel Jct 16/10/37; Pontypool Road 8/20; Severn Tunnel Jct 23/4/49; Barry 28/1/56; Landore 21/2/59; Pontypool Road 27/2/60; withdrawn 6/7/64; mileage at 28/112/63 576,797; sold to J Buttigieg Newport 24/8/64

7231 (5266) 14/12/35; Severn Tunnel Jct 11/1/36; Newport Ebbw Jct 5/2/38; Gloucester 8/40; Newport Ebbw Jct 8/41; Barry 8/9/62; Cardiff Radyr 11/7/63; Llanelly 8/8/63; withdrawn 9/10/64; mileage at 28/12/63 (525,621; sold to Steel Supply Co Jersey Marine Swansea

7232 (5267) 28/8/35; Severn Tunnel jct 21/9/35; Llanelly 3/43; Pontypool Road 22/3/47; Severn Tunnel Jct 23/4/49; Cardiff Canton 9/9/50; Newport Ebbw Jct 17/5/52; Llanelly 21/2/59; Newport Ebbw Jct 11/8/62; Barry 11/7/63; Llanelly 28/11/63; withdrawn 21/5/65; mileage at 28/12/63 519,876; sold to Birds Bynea 24/6/65

7233 (5268) 5/9/35; Pontypool Road 21/9/35; Newport Ebbw Jct 15/6/57; Severn Tunnel Jct 13/6/63; Pontypool Road 31/10/63; withdrawn 7/9/64; mileage at 28/12/63462,617; sold to J Cashmore Newport 14/10/64

7234 (5269) 7/9/35; Oxley 21/9/35; Neath 11/12/38; Pontypool Road 24/1/48; Newport Ebbw Jct 15/6/57; Aberdare 29/12/62; withdrawn 22/10/63; mileage 559,773; sold to R S Hayes Bridgend 1/1/64

7235 (5270) 1/1936; Pontypool Road 8/2/36; Llanelly 30/11/57; Worcester 19/4/58 [on loan]; Gloucester 29/11/58; Duffryn Yard 26/12/59; Llanelly 3/12/60; withdrawn 20/4/64; mileage at 28/12/63 487,924; sold to Birds Morriston 3/6/64

7236 (5271) 1/1936; Oxley 8/2/36; Banbury 13/11/37; Stafford Road 29/4/39; Banbury 27/5/39; Leamington Spa 3/42; Worcester 26/2/49; Newton Abbot 21/4/51; St Blazey 9/8/52; Landore 1/11/52; Banbury 18/6/60; withdrawn 13/11/63; mileage 737,718; sold to A King Norwich 27/1/64

7237 (5272) 1/1936; Oxley 7/3/36; Stafford Road 28/5/38; Oxley 26/6/38; Llanelly 10/12/38; St Philips Marsh 17/5/47; Leamington Spa 24/1/48; Severn Tunnel Jct 12/7/52; Banbury 13/6/59; Aberdare 5/9/59; Carmarthen 17/6/61; Newport Ebbw Jct 4/11/61; Llanelly 29/12/62; withdrawn 17/6/63; mileage 556,919; cut up 7/9/63

7238 (5273) 2/1936; Banbury 7/3/36; Oxley 22/2/47; Duffryn Yard 21/2/53; Oxford 11/7/53; Oxley 3/12/60; Worcester 4/11/61; Newport Ebbw Jct 30/12/61; Barry 11/7/63; withdrawn 20/4/64; mileage at 28/12/63 530,195; sold to Birds Risca 3/6/64

7239 (5274) 2/1936; Banbury 7/3/36; Severn Tunnel Jct 8/41; Oxford 11/7/53; Neath 8/9/62; Cardiff Radyr 6/10/62; Llanelly 1/12/62; withdrawn 22/10/63; mileage 548,432; sold to R S Hayes Bridgend

7240 (4239) 8/1937; Newport Ebbw Jct 18/9/37; Llanelly 8/41; Oxley 9/8/47; Worcester 26/2/49; Newton Abbot 21/4/51; Duffryn Yard 29/11/52; Llanelly 5/9/53; Newport Ebbw Jct 17/5/58; Pontypool Road 13/6/63; withdrawn 7/9/64; mileage at 28/12/63 585,585; sold to J Cashmore Newport 14/10/64

7241 (4220) 9/1937; Newport Ebbw Jct 16/10/37; Swindon 12/41; Newport Ebbw Jct 10/43; St Philips Marsh 24/4/54; Duffryn Yard 23/4/55; Barry 28/1/56; Pontypool Road 8/8/59; withdrawn 26/12/62; mileage 491,131; cut up 29/12/62

7242 (4202) 9/1937; Aberdare 13/1/37; Newport Pill 11/44; Aberdare 2/45; Cardiff Radyr 27/1/51; Llanelly 11/7/63; withdrawn 8/6/64; mileage at 28/12/63 561,039; sold to Birds Morriston 18/8/64

7243 (4204) 1/1938; Swindon 8/1/38; Neath 10/12/38; Oxley 14/6/47; Newport Ebbw Jct 29/11/52; Duffryn Yard 15/7/61; Carmarthen 24/3/62; Barry 19/5/62; Duffryn Yard 26/1/63; Neath 13/4/64; withdrawn 24/7/64; mileage at 28/12/63 531,684; sold to Birds Morriston 4/9/64

7244 (4216) 3/1938; Llanelly 30/4/38; Pantyffynon 26/6/38; Landore 9/8/47; Llanelly 11/8/51; Duffryn Yard 1/12/51; Banbury 30/1/60; Neath 12/8/61; Swansea East Dock 21/4/62; Llanelly 3/11/62; Neath 13/4/64; Llanelly 5/10/64; withdrawn 6/2/65; mileage at 28/12/63 506,852; sold to R S Hayes Bridgend 5/3/65

7245 (4205) 5/1938; Newport Ebbw Jct 28/5/38; Aberbeeg 23/2/63; Cardiff Radyr 24/2/64; withdrawn 7/9/64; mileage at 28/12/63 422,099; sold to R S Hayes Bridgend 14/10/64

7246 (4234) 7/1938; Newport Ebbw Jct 20/8/38; Gloucester 6/43; Severn Tunnel Jct 29/12/45; Oxford 11/7/53; Newport Ebbw Jct 16/6/56; Pontypool Road 22/2/58; withdrawn 30/9/63; mileage 495,755; sold to R S Hayes Bridgend 1/1/64

7247 (4244) 9/1938; Neath 17/9/38; Newport Ebbw Jct 10/43; Leamington Spa 10/7/48; Newport Ebbw Jct 25/12/48; Oxley 26/2/55; Banbury 23/4/60; Neath 15/7/61; Aberdare 29/12/62; withdrawn 22/3/63; mileage 454,879; sold to J Cashmore Newport 18/9/63

7248 (4249) 10/1938; Newport Ebbw Jct 15/10/38; Llanelly 8/41; Oxley 17/5/47; Worcester 26/2/49; Neath 21/4/51; Swansea East Dock 29/11/52; Landore 26/2/55; Duffryn Yard 14/6/57; Swansea East Dock 25/1/58; Danygraig 21/3/59; Swansea East Dock 27/2/60; Neath 29/12/62; Swansea East Dock 23/3/63; Landore 31/12/63; withdrawn 16/6/65; mileage at 28/12/63 534,980; sold to Steel Supply Co. Briton Ferry 28/7/65

7249 (4209) 11/1938; Newport Ebbw Jct 10/12/38; Oxford 24/4/54; Cardiff Cathays 22/5/54; Newport Ebbw Jct 19/6/54; Cardiff Cathays 1/1/55; Duffryn Yard 23/4/55; Severn Tunnel Jct 8/10/60; Newport Ebbw Jct 28/11/64; Cardiff East Dock 10/4/65; Llanelly 15/5/64; withdrawn 16/6/65; mileage at 28/12/63 475,242; sold to Steel Supply Co. Briton Ferry 28/7/65

7250 (4219) 2/1939; Swansea East Dock 1/4/39; newton Abbot 22/2/47; St Philips Marsh 14/6/52; Worcester 30/11/57; Newport Ebbw Jct 27/12/57; Severn Tunnel Jct 24/2/62; Cardiff Radyr 11/8/62; withdrawn28/9/64; mileage at 28/12/63 512,492; sold to R S Hayes Bridgend 27/10/64

7251 (4240) 3/1939; Severn Tunnel Jct 29/4/39; Llanelly 30/11/57; Pontypool Road 19/4/58; Aberdare 3/10/63; withdrawn 6/1/64; mileage at 28/12/63 509,605; cut up 13/4/64

7252 (4210) 4/1939; Newport Ebbw Jct 27/5/39; Didcot 15/6/46; Newport Ebbw Jct 30/10/48; Oxford 24/4/54; Cardiff Cathays 22/5/54; Newport Ebbw Jct 19/6/54; Cardiff Cathays 1/1/55; Barry 23.4.55; Cardiff Radyr 8/8/59; Duffryn Yard 11/7/63; Neath 13/4/64; Severn Tunnel Jct 9/1/65; withdrawn 16/6/65; mileage at 28/12/63 501,398; sold to Steel Supply Co. Briton Ferry 28/7/65

7253 (4245) 12/1939; Newport Ebbw Jct 6/1/40; Swindon 3/42; Newport Ebbw Jct 10/43; Llanelly 13/6/63; Aberdare 24/12/63; Newport Ebbw Jct 6/3/65; Severn Tunnel Jct 10/4/65; withdrawn 30/4/65; mileage at 28/12/63 424,279; sold to Birds Risca 2/6/65

Health Warning
You can never be *entirely* sure of any allocation list; there are official errors, official oversights, official omissions and official blind eyes-turned to lead us astray. On top of that may lurk simple transcription errors; worse, sometimes engines that were at 'outstations' (sub-sheds we called them in later years) weren't recorded as such, while sometimes they were. So they'd be listed under the parent shed. St Blazey was another case; its turntable was out of use during 1952 and as the year wore out 7200, 7236 and 7240 were noted 'still on loan' in place of tender engines. The first two were officially noted going there, 7240 was not. You'll not find Salisbury in the above list but *The Railway Observer* lists its allocation at 7/5/39 as: '4-4-0s 3364, 3396; 2-6-0s 5311, 6303, 7316; 4-6-0 6850 Cleeve Grange; 2-8-0 2841; 0-6-0T 8747, 2-8-2Ts 7210, 7231...' adding the comment 'The allocation given is two or three more than the number of engines usually in the shed on a Sunday.'

7201 in green, brand new as it were, parked on Swindon running shed on 1 September 1934, more or less its first time in daylight following conversion from 5276. GREAT WESTERN in serif, short bonnet, no grab irons on boiler side yet. ColourRail

7200 at the end of the process of transformation from 2-8-0T 5275, at Swindon in July 1934. This is how the original bunker looked, with lamp recess but no 'wind shield' as the crews called it. The sloping rivet line marking the floor of the coal space/ top of the water tank runs *beneath* the number plate and the side and rear hand rails are separate. This bunker held six tons of coal, way more than the four tons or more of a 2-8-0T and 2,500 gallons. It was the type adopted for the first two batches, 7200-7239 but one or two, inexplicably, got the later style of bunker applied to 7240-7253. This type is illustrated with 7242 next. Rail Photoprint

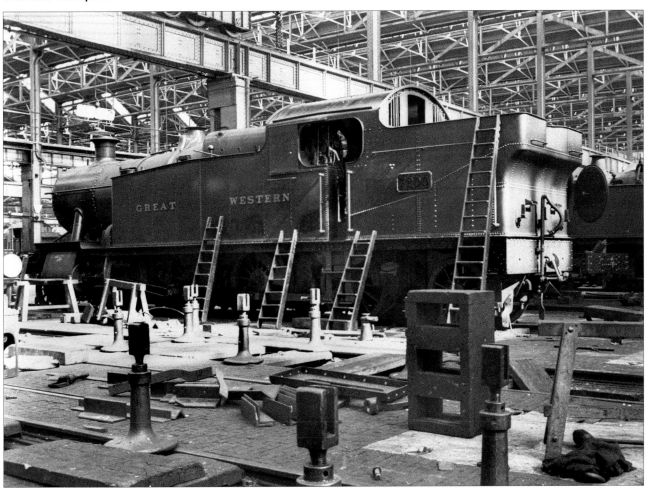

7242, one of the final batch 7240-7253, newly outshopped in BR black with second emblem, at Newport about 1960. The bunker on these held only five tons but the water tank was enlarged to take 2,700 gallons. Note, as a result, how much deeper the bunker lies beneath the lamp recess, while the sloping rivet line now runs *above* the number plate and the top hand rails are wrapped around the bunker rear. Michael Boakes Collection.

7225 carrying a serif version of BRITISH RAILWAYS and typically with old timber mineral wagons, clumps into Cardiff General from the east on the down through road, 28 August 1948. H.C. Casserley, courtesy R.M. Casserley.

2-8-2T at work 1. 7252 powers through a cold Newport (some snow still on the ground) past another train of minerals in the 1960s. RailOnline

2-8-2T at work 2. 7221 with an eastbound ballast through Newport in 1958. It was one of the two in the 7220-7239 batch that late in life were given the latest type front ends – the other one was 7228. Norman Preedy.

Block BRITISH RAILWAYS on 7247 at Swindon, 4 February 1951. R.H. Fullagar, transporttreasury

7225 Stafford Road works, 9 May 1954. This is a 'Heavy-Intermediate' at a guess; the way the boiler sat, with the low coupled axles, it was possible to get at most parts without taking it off the frames. However as the lagging is largely in place, presumably it did not need much attention in any event. A. Price, ColourRail

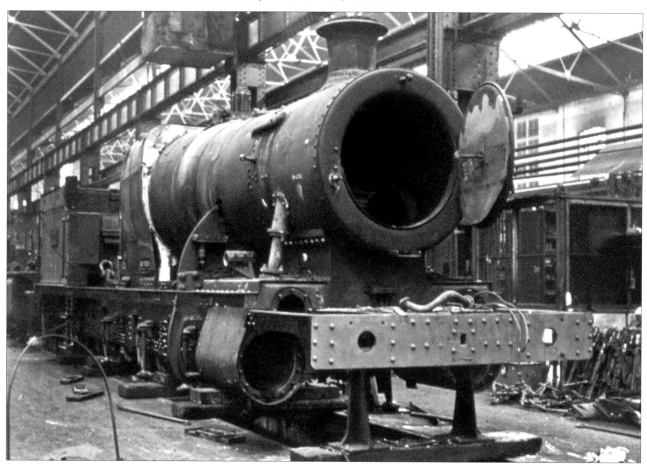

A well-lit 7203 inside a roundhouse – almost certainly a guess at 'somewhere in South Wales' would prove right. First emblem, about 1955; it has collected an inordinate number of lamps on the (non-spare lamp iron) side which will doubtless be distributed amongst its compatriots around the turntable.

2-8-2T at work 3. 7238 with hoppers amidst the largely rural environs of Aberbeeg, 1963. A.E. Durrant, Michael Boakes Collection.

Aberdare's 7203 newly overhauled with BR second emblem at Caerphilly works about 1959 – the course of the ATC conduit can be clearly followed from buffer beam to cab. That looks very much like a polished brass bonnet, with which Caerphilly famously despatched a number of 2-8-2Ts. For all the cleaning that would have gone on, they might just as well have not bothered, and painted them black like other works did. On one or two locos in this section, as here, a second footstep has appeared on the tank fronts; this appears to be a more or less random feature. Some repetition is unavoidable in a series such as these *Papers*, so here goes: *On the right-hand side of some GWR classes (the majority of the GWR 4-cylinder and 2-outside cylinder tender locomotives in fact) there was a long, prominent pipe behind the hand rail, immediately in front of the right-hand cab window. This was the 4-cone ejector. At the back of this substantial pipe was a clack-box, connecting the ejector to the vacuum train pipe. There were also connections to the ejector from the drivers brake valve (DBV) supplying steam to the four cones which created the vacuum. The mixture of steam and air from the train pipe was ejected along the pipe to the smokebox and finally ejected through an annular ring around the base of the chimney into the atmosphere. The drivers brake valve associated with the 4-cone ejector was fitted on to a blank pad on the boiler back plate. In addition to the butterfly valve, which the driver operated to admit air into the train pipe to apply the brake, the DBV incorporated a large, quick action steam valve, which supplied steam from the boiler to the four cones in the ejector to give quick acting evacuation of the train pipe. There was also a small, quick action, steam valve which supplied steam to one of the four cones in the ejector. This was used to maintain the train pipe vacuum when the vacuum pump was not in operation; for example, during station stops. The Manors, 2-6-0s and the tanks however were different, having single cone ejectors. With this arrangement the steam cone was incorporated in the drivers brake valve and the exhaust pipe to the smokebox passed through the boiler to the annular ring under the chimney. This was internal, so there was no prominent pipe along the boiler behind the hand rail; it was made of copper, in contrast to the steel fire tubes. All the vacuum braked tank locomotives were fitted with the single cone ejector; hence no ejector pipe visible on the right-hand side, or visible anywhere for that matter. The DBV in this case had the standard butterfly valve but only had the single large quick action steam valve which supplied steam to the single cone. At sheds, renewal of the steel fire tubes was carried out by the boilersmiths but by some long-forgotten ruling of ancient demarcation, renewal of the copper ejector internal pipe was the responsibility of the fitting staff. This was quite an interesting job because after collapsing and removing the old pipe the new pipe had to be manoeuvred through the tube plate hole and threaded over the boiler tubes towards the corresponding hole in the back plate. Steel fire tubes were rigid but the copper internal pipe was more supple and sagged considerably so it was usually necessary to 'fish' for the end of the pipe with a broom handle, or other such sophisticated device, and guide it through the back plate hole. The pipe was expanded into the back plate and tube plate, to make a steam tight joint and the expanding rollers had to be borrowed from the boilersmiths to do this.* J.B. Lee, ColourRail

7220, with what must have been G W R assiduously expunged. The date and location is not recorded but the distinctive chimney pots of the terrace in the background reveal it to be Newton Abbot – they're still there! 7220, oddly, has the GW shed code NA stencilled on the cylinder (twice!) and it was indeed operating from there from 1947-1952, with a spell at St Blazey in between. Michael Boakes Collection.

7211 in the dullest of grime-grey livery and bereft of apparent ownership as befits the period, at Swansea East Dock on 6 July 1947, with the recent 'modern' replacement coal stage very much in the style of the original in the background. 7211 has no tank top lubricator but did get them subsequently – see it next in 1955, page 17. It has the levelling pipe behind the cab steps here and the taller form of tank ventilator, unlike in the next picture over a decade later. H.C. Casserley, courtesy R.M. Casserley.

The horizontal tank weld line makes its appearance on a very different-looking 7211, fresh out at Swindon and alongside the Reception Shed, on 10 August 1955. On top of the sloping part of the tank between the clack feeds to the bonnet and the shoulder of the firebox is an oblong component appearing to sit on four 'legs'. This is the lubricator, an oil tray with feed running behind the tanks to the axleboxes. It was used on many of the Big Prairies but not on the 2-8-0T predecessors of the 7200s. They were not original but appeared some time after the engines' introduction. After 7219 the lubricator was repositioned and disappeared from the tank top, while in some instances they were removed from 7200-7219. It looks like a new sliding shutter, without the coat of glossy paint, was put on at the last minute. J. Robertson, transporttreasury

2-8-2T at work 4. 7236, while not quite at work then clearly ready for work, sitting at the back of Banbury shed about 1961. A lovely, homely portrait. Something about that old oil drum, the hut and the junk makes you want to model it... RailOnline

7200 leaves Brent Loop with an up goods, of mainly elderly wagons, on 18 January 1951. 7200 carried at the end and into its long stay at Woodhams yard (and still does in its ongoing restoration) the 'second' bunker (as fitted to 7240-7253 from the first) with the curve in the rear panel much lower and the rivet line *above* the number plate. It kept however the original disposition of the hand rails. The rivet line on 7200 in fact can be plotted, varying from one position to the other through the 1950s. What this means is unclear. It hardly seems credible that a decision was made to increase the water capacity on this particular engine and two or three others with all the work that entailed. Presumably repairs were made using material that was to hand, and the plate forming the coal space floor/water tank top as used on the third batch was the only one available. The cab roof rainstrip on 7200-7219 generally sloped upwards towards the back of the roof. A. Lathey, transporttreasury

7201 at Pontypool Road, 16 October 1960. It too has the 'second' bunker as fitted to 7240-7253, indicated by the rivet line running above the number plate and the bunker rear curving about a foot lower. It also has the 'wind shield' above the lamp recess, a feature 7200 also acquired. Ken Fairey, ColourRail

7202 having come a bit of a cropper, is being re-railed in Barry Docks yard on 11 July 1963. This is the original style of bunker, in which there was more coal, but less water. The curve at the rear is only about the depth of the lamp recess and the rivet line runs *below* the number plate, albeit with a slight kink. Peter Skelton.

A more dignified 7202, at Salisbury on 24 May 1961; the 88B plate at this time indicates Radyr. The small upright bottle object in front of the tank is the 'class B' vacuum pump lubricator. It supplied oil to the pump cylinder to lubricate the pump piston. Ken Fairey, ColourRail

7203 with a down freight at Park Junction, Newport, on 7 April 1954. D.K. Jones Collection.

7203 newly outshopped at Caerphilly Works (we saw it there in the *Introductory Notes* too, pages 14-15) in 1959, showing to advantage the original bunker of the 7200-7239 engines, with the rivet line below the number plate. Note again Caerphilly's trademark burnished safety valve bonnet. S.B. Lee, ColourRail

7204 in the anonymous condition typical of the period, at Didcot on 16 August 1947. There were four of the big tanks at Didcot, 7214, 7228 and 7252 arriving in June-July 1946 and 7204 arriving in March 1947. All were transferred away in October 1948 but what their role at Didcot was (it must have been a specific, heavy one) is not clear. They are said to have been used on general freight traffic towards Reading and London but there was a large Central Ordnance Depot at Didcot on the site later occupied by the power station. This would have generated substantial heavy traffic, particularly during the war, and would have tailed off afterwards, matching the movement of the locos. H.C. Casserley, courtesy R.M. Casserley.

7204 at Reading shed, with a 2-8-0T behind, on 28 April 1963.(We know it's a 2-8-0T not a 2-8-2T from additional photographs taken the same day.) Eight coupled tanks of either ilk were irregular visitors to Reading. Local driver Roy Williams (*Ten Years at 81D*, notes by Nick Deacon, *British Railways Illustrated, passim*) fired a couple of 7200s and reckoned them 'the worst' ex-GWR type he ever worked on. Perhaps it was a matter of unfamiliarity! Ken Fairey, ColourRail

7205 back in its native haunts, at Bargoed on 1 July 1963 with Target H33; these are empties and the train will be northbound for collieries in the Rhymney valley or to the east. That will be South box in the distance. Like others, 7205 kept a single footstep at the tank front to the end. ColourRail

A contrast around the Swindon Works turntable, where newly outshopped locos reposed after a trial run, 27 September 1959; sometimes quite a few adjustments would be necessary as parts were found to be heating up or whatever. 7205, shimmering in black, will go home to 88A Cardiff Cathays while 46520, clearly in green but without a shed plate as yet, will also be going to Wales, to Oswestry. RailOnline.

7205 at Chippenham, on its way home. Bunker tank vent pipe visible on back of cab. Michael Boakes Collection.

Two sides of the 7205 coin; firstly at Radyr on 1 June 1963. In the *Introductory Notes*, a side-on picture of the loco served to illustrate the position and function of the water levelling pipe, behind the cab steps yet clearly here, many years on, it is gone. It turns out that on both the 2-8-0 and 2-8-2Ts they were prone to fracturing. The pipe had to come off (no quick and easy procedure by any means) for the break to be welded with the loco out of service until it had been refitted and the tanks refilled. An 'experimental armoured hose levelling pipe' was arrived at in 1952 and by 1954 the new arrangement and the consequent removal of the visible pipes was underway amongst the two classes. The process did not go unnoticed by a correspondent to *The Railway Observer: The cast-iron water equalising pipes connecting bunker and side tanks on the 2-8-0Ts are being replaced by fabricated elbow pipes joined by thick india-rubber hoses. 4276, 5206 and 5244 have been altered together with 2-8-2T 7225.*

Still at Radyr, now side by side with EE Type 3s, on 30 August 1964. The WR route availability/power group disc tended to migrate about a bit on various engines. On the right-hand side of 7205 (top picture) it is somewhat high, on the left-hand side, here, it is more central between the number plate and the hand rail. Ken Fairey, ColourRail

7206 runs east through Pyle station on the South Wales main line with up tankers; we are looking west from the footbridge at Pyle on 13 August 1962. Down main platform on left (with three seated 'spotters) and up main on right with the bridge carrying the A48 Cardiff-Carmarthen road in the background. On the right-hand side is the little loading bank, goods lock-up and cattle pens. The single line branch to Waterhall Junction on the Ogmore Vale Extension line (which ran from Margam Junction to Tondu) curves away past these buildings on the right. This branch closed in September 1963. The connecting line in the right foreground served three dead-end sidings on the other side of the Up platform. Pyle closed in November 1964 but reopened on a new site about half a mile to the west in 1994. L. Rowe, ColourRail

7208 sits in Severn Tunnel Junction shed yard, about 1960 at a guess. Two steps at tank front and a slightly altered tank vent pipe (it is in two parts) which appeared as standard later on and then filtered down to earlier engines. The clutter on the tank top is frequently augmented by a long fire cleaning shovel, as here, held in place by its own bracket. 7208, along with 7222, had gone to Newton Abbot in the War for banking freights over Dainton, between Newton Abbot and Totnes. They were certainly adding to the gaiety of nations, joining a long list that included Halls, Granges, 2-6-0s, 51XX, 41XX and 61XX 2-6-2Ts and even LMS 8F 2-8-0s, LNER O4 2-8-0s and USA 2-8-0s! ColourRail

7209 at Oxford on 1 June 1962. By now this was the 2-8-2T's home shed. There had been one at Oxford since the early 1950s, and 7226 had briefly been there new in 1935. Most stayed only briefly but one or two for several years. 7209 was the last, going in October 1962. On the left is 6950 KINGSTHORPE HALL. The latter bears an electrification flash, something rarely applied (for quite obvious geographical reasons) to the eight-coupled tanks. ColourRail

Llanelly's 7211 resplendent in BR black, back home in South Wales from overhaul, at Radyr about 1960. The oil pipes to the cylinders and the Swindon design of smokebox-mounted regulator in the superheater header ran out of sight beneath the cladding but were not run through the front tubeplate but instead went outside the boiler barrel and then back in to the smokebox. All that takes place under the oblong cover on the right-hand side, where this piping briefly emerged (there were stopcocks under the cover, with leaks often present, streaking down the smokebox) to span boiler and smokebox. Most 2-8-2Ts by far had the original dart-shaped cover, visible on any number of pictures in this volume so this new pattern indicated alteration to the superheater of 7211 at its latest works visit. To repeat a bit: *Most GW engines had hydrostatic sight feed displacement lubricators mounted in the cab, under the control of the driver. Increased/divided oil supply to valves and pistons meant there was a similar cover on the left-hand side of the smokebox on the tender engines but on most tanks it was concealed, underneath the boiler casing.* ColourRail

7211 at the now dilapidated Pantyffynon shed, 17 April 1964. The engine was withdrawn soon after and the MPD closed shortly after that. The crude 'C' might stand for 'Condemned', with 7211 reprieved for a short while. RailOnline

Another Oxford 2-8-2T, 7212, at Gloucester Horton Road shed on 30 August 1953. Alongside is 2-6-2T 3164. Half a dozen or so 2-8-2Ts were at Gloucester at various times in the Second World War, 'solely' for banking between Gloucester and Bourton on the Water on the Kingham line. One other materialised much later, 7235 in 1958-59. A.R. Carpenter, transporttreasury

7213 at Shrewsbury (the 2-8-2Ts used to work as far as Birkenhead from South Wales) photographed from the island platform at the north end; the loco is on the bi-directional through road. An unusual instance of one bearing the electrification flashes, almost certainly acquired during its time at Oxley, December 1960-December 1962, which provides some idea of the period – the flashes came in after 1960. There are now, for whatever reason, cut-outs in the running plate above the rear buffer. Perhaps it was to give the fireman's boot some extra clearance when he was clambering from buffer stock to footstep. ColourRail

7214 inside Aberdare roundhouse on 6 May 1951. The cab superstructure rested flush against the bunker assembly, with four bolts fixing to a plate welded inside the latter, as here. Repeated overhauls deranged this and an extra plate/bolts were devised, as on 7205 say, pictured earlier at Radyr in 1963-64. Back in 1951 7214 had yet to acquire the horizontal tank weld, and has a patch weld repair by the cab rear. Tank top lubricator prominent, along with inevitable fire shovel. H.C. Casserley, courtesy R.M. Casserley.

7214 at Newport Ebbw Junction MPD, 24 June 1956, with first emblem but now with two lower patch weld repairs on the tankside. This is an indication perhaps of how corrosion in the lower tank eventually led to new parts being welded in, and that marked horizontal line. A circular target board is stowed by the steam pipe. R.J. Buckley, Initial Photographics.

7215 in fairly battered condition about 1947, location unknown. It lacks the vertical boiler grab irons, the cylinder casing has a temporary 'stitch-up', a plug seals a hole near the front of the tank, there is a big patch repair weld at the bottom, the sliding shutter looks to be falling off, the safety valve bonnet and clack covers are barely seated and the washout plug covers are loose; quite why the Western persisted with these fussy little covers is a mystery. No one else used them. Lamp iron still on smokebox top. transporttreasury

Landore's 7217, newly returned from works (Caerphilly by the look of the bonnet) tucked away in the roundhouse at Canton MPD, 21 July 1957. The reflection of the new black paint largely obscures it, but the second emblem *is* there. R. Wilson, transporttreasury

7219 at Salisbury, 1 August 1963; second emblem just about visible, modified tank vent. Rail Photoprint

7220 at Shrewsbury (outside the 'New Shed' – the 'Old Shed' is to the right) at an unknown date; all we know is that it carries the 86G of Pontypool Road, where the loco was allocated, from September 1954 right through to withdrawal, and before about 1959-60 by which time it might be expected to have acquired the second emblem. The first of the 7220 series, it took, like the others in the batch 7220-7239, the straight running plate over the cylinders together with the square drop ends of the original 2-8-0Ts. Cab roof rainstrip on 7220-7239 was horizontal and positioned directly above cab opening. transporttreasury

The east end of the Reception Shed at Swindon Works, with 7221 freshly part-painted in BR black with first emblem, 25 April 1954. 7221 has got new cylinders, so now has the raised running plate and curved drops either side. The tender of a new BR 77000 2-6-0 is visible between 7221 and an adjacent pannier tank.

7221, now much-begrimed, at Gloucester Horton Road MPD on 23 September 1964. It is a Banbury engine now, on the LMR carrying a 2D plate. There were no exceptions allowed on the LM it seems, and the electrification flashes have appeared on 7221. It was withdrawn a few weeks later. Peter Skelton.

7222 rumbles through Glyn Neath in 1964; there's all sorts of welded patchwork going on low down in the bunker water tank. No cut outs in running plate at rear, as noted on 7213. RailOnline

7222, obviously not long out of overhaul at Swindon, at Ebbw Junction on 7 August 1961. Its official allocation there came some weeks later. The two feed oil box at the front of the smokebox saddle is just visible for once. It fed oil to the tops of the two pony truck axleboxes from where it was channelled to lubricate the horn faces. During its last days as an Aberdare engine 7222 carried a distinctive (and distinctly amateur) homemade smokebox number plate – the numbers were almost italicised! Norman Preedy.

7224 at Exeter shed where it had been newly allocated, in the summer of 1961. It left for Ebbw Junction at the end of the year and these months constituted the only time it was not working from Welsh sheds. ColourRail

7225 at home, Swansea East Dock shed, August 1961. Oil bottle lodged in window, engine quite smart for a 2-8-2T; an unknown component sits by the tank filler, doubtless left by a fitter. Photographs before and after this show the tanks with two steps at the front rather than the single one here, the tanks clearly changing at intervals as much as did boilers. Norman Preedy.

7226 heads a line of similarly grimy tanks at Swansea East Dock shed about 1963; good view again of the oil tray on the smokebox saddle front, the ATC gear and the way the vacuum pipe disappears under the axle of the pony truck. 7226 moved on after this, to outlast Swansea East Dock shed. A. Scarsbrook, Initial Photographics.

7228 parked while some cylinder parts are attended too – the curved sheeting on the running plate is the casing from the far side cylinder. The item on the floor is the front cylinder cover complete with its pressure relief valve. Notice the ATC shoe under the buffer beam and how close that injector overflow pipe is to the trailing side rod! This was the other one in this series to acquire a modified front end late on. Oddly the date when hasn't been recorded. Peter Skelton.

Ebbw Junction's 7231 running north light engine on the GW Salisbury branch near Heytesbury, 9 July 1938; note how tank vent for the third 'bunker' tank runs along the edge of the bunker to be secured on the cab rear. H.C. Casserley, courtesy R.M. Casserley.

Now at home at Ebbw Junction in the late 1950s, having acquired the ubiquitous horizontal weld line. Michael Boakes Collection.

7231 (now with short bonnet) at a shed where they weren't to be found that often, you'd think. This is Stratford-upon-Avon, a little two road shed with only four or five locos of its own, on 26 June 1960. 7231 has the bunker arrangement original to all the 2-8-2Ts so far, with the rivet line passing below the number plate indicating six tons, 2,500 gallons. Ken Fairey, ColourRail

Now at Pantyfynnon shed, on 22 July 1964. Since June 1960 it has been 're-bunkered', for it now carries the style used on 7240-7253; that is, with a deeper drop before the curve and the rivet line running above the plate. It retains the hand rail arrangement, however, of its bunker's previous incarnation. In theory then, this is now a five ton, 2,700 gallon bunker. L. Turner, transporttreasury

7234 at its home shed, Pontypool Road, 13 September 1953. A few years before, in 1949, *The Railway Observer* noted that 'The 72XX 2-8-2Ts from Pontypool Road spend a lot of time banking up the Cwm incline and shunting. They have never been popular for main line work owing to the frequent stops necessary for water, and with more 2-8-0 tender engines available lead rather quiet lives.' Norman Preedy.

Pontypool Road's poor grime-caked 7235 on 8 April 1951. Underneath it all, outshone by the freestyle chalked triffid, is a serif BRITISH RAILWAYS. Levelling pipe behind the steps (they would not be superseded for a few years), the second type of tank vent (two parts, joined at a substantial flange) and the usual shovels slung on the tank. There's another fire iron poking out of the cab. R.J. Buckley, Initial Photographics.

7236 awaiting attention at Wolverhampton Works on 18 February 1962. It was deemed worthy of overhaul, for it was not withdrawn until the end of 1963. The safety valve bonnet and clack covers have been removed and not for the first time. Back in 1945-46 it had run, peculiarly, for over a year in this condition. Even more remarkably it emerged from overhaul at Swindon in June 1946 (with the safety valve bonnet at last restored incidentally) painted green. RailOnline

7237 at Swindon shed; second emblem, 18 September 1960. Rail Photoprint.

'Re-bunkered' 7239 at Oxford Rewley Road, 15 August 1959. R.C. Riley, transporttreasury

With the third batch, from 7240, the engines had the bunker with not so much coal but more water, denoted by the rivet line running diagonally *above* the number plate, and with the rearward curving part much deeper, as here. Also these engines got the 'modern' style of running plate curved over the cylinders; they were rebuilt from assorted older engines and new front ends/cylinders with outside steam pipes were made for them. In general appearance 7240-7253 resembled 7200-7219. This is 7240 after its final Heavy General, by which time the bunker rivet line was doubled up, and much more prominent. Note how the horizontal hand rail curves around the bunker now... The tank top lubricator seems to have disappeared for good with these engines. Cab roof rainstrip was an inverted 'V' on this batch. Norman Preedy.

7240 at Penrhos Junction, 12 May 1952. That would be Penrhos Junction box at left, Penrhos branch off behind it to eventually join the rest of the branch (closed) running over that viaduct beyond (its piers partly visible). Caerphilly and Pontypridd line to right, line to Taffs Well and Radyr in the middle, upon which 7240 is forging north with empties (all wooden ex-PO wagons) on 12 May 1952. R.C. Riley, transporttreasury

7242 at Radyr shed, 23 June 1957; fading first emblem. Ken Fairey, ColourRail

7242 with a train of new BR steel minerals, at Oldfield Park Bath, 2 December 1961. M. Burch, Michael Boakes Collection.

What must have been the brightest loco on shed, 7242 at Radyr on 12 August 1962. Modellers can never be entirely sure where the horizontal weld line went, where the emblem went, or the relation between them – compare with 7228 on page 37 for instance. L. Rowe, ColourRail

A clean 7243; bereft of lettering or insignia, the period would be the 'hiatus' 1948-51. ColourRail

7244 at Duffryn Yard on 14 September 1959; presumably this is the fork to the west of the shed, with No.1 box and the Port Talbot dock line running off to the left. H.C. Casserley, courtesy R.M. Casserley.

Swansea East Dock's 7244 waits its turn to be traversed into the shops at Swindon in 1962. The modified bunker of the 7240-7253 series had rather different hand rails, swept around the corner, as here. John F. Meakin, transporttreasury

7244 after its overhaul – the period is believed to be August 1962. Diesels lurk in the distance (at left) and note the whitewashed subway entrance; the Hall awaiting works at right is 6916. RailOnline

A pristine 7245 at Ebbw Junction on 5 July 1952. That weld line certainly did not do the emblem transfer any favours. RailOnline

Oxley's 7247 at home, 29 December 1957. It seems never to have had the welded tanks so common with earlier engines; indeed the incidence of 'the weld' is less common in these later engines. Maybe the tanks were made of sterner stuff by now. The rare right-hand facing lion can be discerned in the emblem. Ken Fairey, ColourRail

7248 at Swansea East Dock, still with first emblem, about 1959. Norman Preedy.

Landore's 7248 runs through the west end on the up through road at Cardiff General on 29 August 1964. Chimney of Brains brewery off St Mary's Street in middle distance. 7248 avoided the horizontal weld on the tanks to the end but required a patch about four feet long adjacent to the cab, on both sides. Ken Fairey, ColourRail

7248 near the end of its life, inside Llanelly shed in 1965. Michael Boakes Collection.

A bit battered and in true 'BR Grey', 7249 rests in front of 2-10-0 92214 (now preserved) at Severn Tunnel Junction on 4 September 1964. Bunker piled high with the despised 'eggs' (ruder terms were in regular use). Peter Groom.

7249 has now moved out of the way to a weedy corner at Severn Tunnel Junction to await its next job. Poor old 7249 and the weeds symbolise in a way the shed's last days; engines sat dead and unused while LMR visitors seemed to outnumber the natives at times. Diesels proliferated and a few months on, in 1965, one visitor found only a solitary engine, a Grange, in steam. Both plug covers dangling, typical of neglect in these late days. Peter Groom.

7250 at Ebbw Junction in 1959; first emblem, typically scruffy with its next big overhaul coming up... Rail Photoprint

A year later, where most GW engines got to stand at one time or another, on a spur off the Swindon Works turntable. A beautiful black 7250, Ebbw Junction shed plate picked out in white, on 18 March 1960. The lubricator pipe cover straddling the boiler/smokebox is now much larger and more or less an oblong rather than a dart shape, reflecting differences in the superheater header, inside the smokebox. Not many 7200s saw this development. Note, no horizontal weld. An extreme oddity is that 7250 does not carry a top lamp iron, a short-lived error which briefly came about when a new smokebox door was fitted. At Ebbw the year before (see previous picture) it carried the lamp iron on the door; moreover the bunker back then had the hand rail wrapped around the rear, as originally arranged. 7250 has emerged here with the shorter hand rail of the earlier engines... Norman Preedy.

There was something about 7250... Here it is heading a down goods, leaving Dainton tunnel with class E lamps, indicating a fitted head of leading vans vacuum braked, 1 January 1948. Somebody has over-indulged the Christmas/New Years Eve cheer perhaps, outlining with chalk the number plate, putting a serif on the buffer beam number, and adding a smokebox door number. Our artist has marked BR over the W of the GWR on the tank. Anticipating what was to come, he nearly got it right, bless him! L.F. Folkard, ColourRail

7250 gets empties under way in the Rhymney, at Bargoed in 1964. Proof (here and above) that the lamp iron was reinstated on the door! A.E. Durrant, Michael Boakes Collection.

7251 at Carmarthen shed, 21 April 1959. That weld line/emblem relationship has wandered a little again... David Idle, transporttreasury

7252, anonymous as per the times, at Ebbw Junction shed on 4 May 1951; one of the wartime ash shelters is still in use in the background. H.C. Casserley, courtesy R.M. Casserley.

7252 wanders through Newport on the down through road, Target 406, in January 1960. The down Capitals United Express is held over on the platform line. Ex-3.55pm Paddington, it has arrived at platform 6, apparently having conditional stops not advertised, including Newport. The train indicator number of 730 changed to F55 from the Summer 1960 timetable. J.L. Lean, ColourRail

Hard to resist this one. 7252 is on the turntable at Radyr MPD on 8 February 1961 and someone was obviously looking forward to St Davids Day. Chalked on the smokebox door is a rocket taking off and COUNT DOWN 24 DAYS TO ST DAVIDS DAY; lodged in the hand rail is a leek to let everyone know he means it. RailOnline

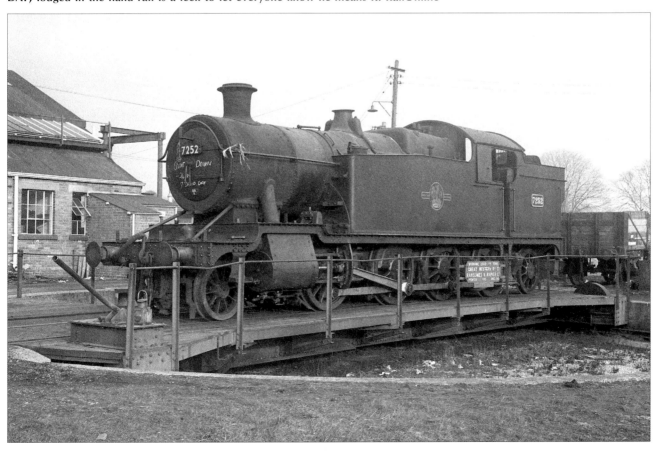

7253, inside Aberdare roundhouse on 4 September 1964. That injector overflow pipe certainly does look perilously close to the coupling rod... Peter Groom.

7253 was withdrawn on 30 April 1965; here it is at Aberdare in its last weeks, still active and undergoing attention; the safety valve bonnet is off and is perched on the firebox top. Derek Short, courtesy Peter Skelton